Rebel Poet

A LIFETIME IN VERSE

SARAH CROWNE

Cover design by Kelsey Gietl. Cover image from The Metropolitan Museum of Art Open Access collection.

For permission requests, write to the author at the address below.

Sarah Crowne

whatsgoinonslnpublishing@gmail.com

First edition 2026

ISBN (Paperback) 979-8-9958164-0-9

ISBN (e-book) 979-8-9958164-1-6

Library of Congress Control Number: 2026910520

https://sarahcrownebooks.com

To my children and future generations:
Life is journey. Go out and live it.

I left my heart here, bleeding on the floor—
only so I could mend it back together again.

— SARAH CROWNE

The Journey of a Poet

Poetry is the soul's heartbeat. Between stanzas we find ourselves—reaching, hoping, waiting—trying to make sense of our hearts, the world, and those we love. Poetry is the song of life.

It's easy to forget what it means to live. We spend our days busy, beaten down by algorithms, current events, struggles, and fears. Trapped in senseless things that steal our attention and harden our hearts. We dwell in stories of who we once were. Forget how far we've come.

These poems were never meant to be a collection. They were written over the span of a life—from age thirteen to now, in my forties. They were scribbled in notebooks and journals, typed on word processors, laptops and desktops, and on scrap pieces of paper. I wrote them in moments of wonder, grief, rebellion, heartbreak, and hope.

Together, they form a map: decades of growth, the becoming of a woman. What it means to be human. A thread we can all connect to.

While I plot my novels, I've never structured my poetry. I let it live. Breathe. It comes to me like a gift—a song on the wind, pulsing in my heart. Born in verse, delivered by God and angels.

Each poem and prayer helps me uncover who I am. I'm still learning. Still growing. Still failing. Still rising.

Compiling this collection has been its own journey. Reflecting on work written as young as age 13 has been a trip. I've scoured through hundreds of poems, discovered lost ones I forgot I'd written, and felt inspired to write new ones after a period of not writing any.

This is by far the most personal work I've shared to date. While I've edited for typos and spelling, I've left the poems raw—not changing anything from their original form—left exactly the same as the day I wrote them. I've separated the poems into decades and noted my age, if I remembered it.

Artists take risks. This is mine. My hope is that you find something here that resonates. Inspires. Settles in your heart. And if nothing else, I'm sharing it for the young girl who etched her heart in ink—all the while praying one day her words would change the world.

I hope you recognize something of your own in these poems. A moment you once lived. A feeling you once carried. A version of yourself that you once were. A story you are ready to let go of.

Thank you for walking through these years with me.
Sarah Crowne

Teen Spirit

Encouraging Words

Your words
create me.
They give me
spirit
and life
warmth
and shelter.
With your encouraging words,
I can reach the sky
I can dance the clouds
to my fullest ability.
But I can only do this if your words are true.
For if they are not,
I will swell inside
and the seed you have planted
will extend from its roots,
overpowering my soul
with its poisonous stem.
I will die
from your poisonous words.
So speak to me
only with the the goodness of your heart.
Raise me
to touch the stars
and I shall reward you
with some encouraging words.

- Age 13 and Winner of the National Kerman
*   High California's 1995 Poetry Anthology*
*   Contest.*

My Imagination

It's a place of wonder,
filled with the unknown,
a place of dreams
and a place of hope.
Where my fears hide
behind a wall,
my thoughts collide,
my spirit calls.
It's where I climb the highest mountain
or swim across the sea.
Anything is possible here—
if you believe.
I can reach the sky
and dance among the clouds;
like a bird, I soar.
This place is my imagination,
a place of forevermore.

Age 14

Mr. Raindrop

Mr. Raindrop—
beating on my windowpane,
how far have you fallen—
to be here today?

You give rhythm
to the winds' howling song.
Your pitter-patter
helps the trees
to dance along.

Mr. Raindrop
have you ever seen the sun,
and the rainbow created
when you become one?

I'm not sure you know
Mr. Raindrop,
how important you are—
on keeping the world green and new
from here
to corners far.

You're sad and lonely,
falling gently from the sky.
Didn't you know, Mr. Raindrop?
We need you.
You help give us life.

Mr. Raindrop,
beating on my windowpane.

How far have you fallen
to be here today?

You say you've never seen the sun.
But I say that's not true—

Go on, you'll see.
He's waiting with a rainbow—
just for you.

-Age 14

Bones

*You are bones
Covered with flesh
And skin to hold you in.
You are nerves
And cells
And organs
A heart that beats.
But that is not all you are.*

*You are essence
A soul, a purpose
Despite how you may appear
What you are
Is who you are
In dim lights
And reactions to fear.*

You are not merely bones.

*You are a purpose
A being of life
From which
A breeze of breath
God breathed into you
To pursue this journey
To make you—*

ALIVE.

- Age 15

Criticism of the Blood

I'm sorry I don't believe in myself.
But I do not.
Just why,
I don't know.
It was nothing said
or done
by you,
that brought me these uncontrollable
thoughts of
failure.

They say
days passed
become
tomorrow's scars.
Maybe somewhere,
sometime,
criticism caused me
to give up hope.

But you see,
it's all so frustrating.
no one understand my fear of failure,
my fear of success.

I have been thought to be an angel
I have been thought to be
something wonderful,
someone silly,
someone caring,
By all those that are my friend.

Maybe I just don't take well—
to the criticism of the blood.

Maybe I just pretend,
or wear a mask to those
who know me.
Maybe I'm just
riding this roller coaster
of adolescence,
Where I
am my own worst enemy,
My own foe.
Who knows?

But just the same,
something is there,
invisible,
but identifiable by me.

Maybe for once
I should do for myself,
With no fear—
And no holding back.

Maybe I just need to learn to accept,
Criticism of the blood.

- Age 15. This poem was the first poem I ever published nationally. I remember sitting in my high school library feeling like I was bleeding my emotions on the page. It was writing this poem that helped me work through my fear of failure and submit my work. It appeared in *The High School Writer* in 1995, earning me a Writer's Merit Award from the publication.

Face In a Tree

One time I thought I saw
a face in a tree
with crazy eyes,
he was staring at me.
And he asked me—
to spite his curiosity:

"Little girl, where are you going?
Why are you crying?
Why are you so sad?"

And I sat and I wondered, and I said:

"I have a scar where I
scraped my knees—
and on my two scraped elbows…
a result of slipping
on broken dreams.
And it stings
Oh, how it stings."

And that one time,
I thought I saw that face in a tree,
with his crazy eyes—
watching me.
He told me
in an attempt to cure my sting:

"Little girl, I know where you're going.
I know why you are crying—
and why you look so sad.

*You cry over scraped elbows and knees
and say, "Oh how it stings!"
But you are forgetting
the most important thing:*

*Only by falling will you know how to stand.
Only by scraped knees will you build yourself
strong.
You say you have patience—
but you are always in
too much of a hurry
to stop and learn.
You may sting
but only by the sting
can you avoid the burn."*

*Oh, that crazy tree.
Too smart for his own good.*

- Age 15

Trashy Tabloid Magazine

Trashy tabloid magazine
Sitting on my table
Think I'll read
My trashy tabloid magazine.

A 90-year-old woman pregnant
A famous punk is dead
And a boy was born with three heads.
Elvis at the mall
I think it said.

Creature somewhere from the unknown
Shook hands with the Pope.
You don't believe it? Take a read!
It's all right here,
In my trashy tabloid magazine.

They say this year
A big earthquake
And dinosaur bones found in
the Great Lakes.
5000 pound woman runs a marathon—
All the way from Boston to Milan!

Crazy world—
So much happening every day.
But don't you worry
Superman will save us,
so they say.

Oh, trashy tabloid magazine

Why do you write things so unseen?
Do you think we are dumb?
Maybe we are . . .
We keep buying you—
From The Sun to Star!

Oh trashy tabloid magazine,
Please don't write a scoop on me.
I think I'll throw you away.

This inquiring mind no longer wants to know.

- Age 15

Simple Things

"I've been thinking about simple things,"
he said.
"Like singing in the rain and—
tea on Tuesday.
Simple things,
like smiling
and waking up
to watch the sun rise.
Remember?
Wishing on stars,
dancing in your bedroom
with the door closed
your hairbrush, the microphone?
Being seven and believing
Santa Claus exists.
Simple things."

"And I've been dreaming about simple days,"
he said.
"Days like Easter,
when your biggest task
was to find your basket of candy.
Days of laughing,
running, jumping,
pretending.
Remember?
Looking at your ceiling
as you lie on your bed
wondering,
what will I grow up to be?
Where will I live?

What will I look like?
Will I be rich and famous?
I never thought to dream of being healthy,"
he said.

The room grew silent
as I waited for him to give his final reply.
He lowered his head and softly said,
"I've been wishing for a simple world.
A simple, beautiful world.
Where angels sing from every corner of the sky.
Where the rain keeps rhythm with the wind
and the sun dances happily along.
Where the complicated complications of
this world
do not exist.
I've been wishing—"

(He pauses as if to find the strength to continue)

"That AIDS was a simple thing."

- Age 16. I wrote this after meeting a person
*   with HIV in High School Health Class around*
*   1995. His story touched me deeply, so I*
*   wrote this poem.*

Spare Change

I saw a man,
on the sidewalk.
He stood there,
holding his
empty coffee cup—
that collected everyone else's
spare change.

His fingers were tarnished with dirt,
his hair—
nasty with grime.
It hung there,
crude and coarse.

As I walked past,
he called out to me,
"Miss, do you have any spare change?"

I kept walking,
then I paused.

His voice had been so empty.

I reached into my pocket
and found,
some spare change.
I turned back to face him,
and dropped my fifty cents
into his coffee cup bank.

*Each quarter made a chiming sound
as it fell into his cup.*

"God bless you child," he replied.

*I noticed he had only two
yellow front teeth.*

*I turned to walk away,
but then—
he called out my name.
I was scared.
Heart pounding.
How did he know me?*

*"Don't be frightened child," he said.
"I will not harm you."*

*I turned around
and faced him once more.
Only now–
his grubby appearance
was gone.*

He was beautiful.

*Bright as the sun,
and as peaceful
as the early morning hours,
of a new day.*

*I felt like I knew him.
I felt safe.
I had never felt such a*

feeling of ease.

He was an angel.
My guardian angel.

"Thanks for the spare change," my angel said.

I wondered why an angel would thank me
for change.

As if he could read my mind he answered:

"You have not let appearance or
poverty influence you.
My child you have given
to whom you thought was in need.
For this you will be blessed."

Then, he gave me a smile,
and vanished—
leaving me on the sidewalk
as the people passed.
Not one witnessing the miracle
that I had just seen
all for one reason.

I had been kind enough to give my spare
change.

- Age 16.

Author Note: This poem won first place in the
Imagery category of the National Kerman
High 1995 Poetry contest. Being from New

England, I was very excited to win a national contest out of California. I was gifted a journal and an award. Also, I wrote this poem after an encounter with a man on the sidewalks of Boston during my first trip to the city.

I Promise

Do not cry when I am gone.
Smile and remember my face—
my laughter and my voice.
The touch of my hand,
my breath on your face.

Be happy for me—
I have gone to live with the Lord!
We will see one another again—
in the blink of an eye,
as quick as the sun
touches the sky
at dawn.

Be glad that God has taken me,
that my mission on earth is complete.
Do not worry about yourselves.
I will be watching over you—
I promise.

Just know that I lived.
That I ran and I played
I won and I lost
smiled and cried.
Know that I love you.
Remember those simple things.
Do not cry,
because I will be waiting for you in heaven.
I promise.

- Age 16

Silver Rain

Silver rain,
falling gently from the sky,
disillusion me
once again tonight.
Silver rain.

Silver rain,
my love laughs at the sky;
he says fate is laughing too,
but not I.

I know destiny is on her way.
Silver rain,
silver rain?

Garden of Always

My garden of always
was blooming some maybes,
and promises were promising
they'd bloom sometime in June.

Blue blanket skies—
we were laughing.
You said you heard fate laughing too.
And I said
hope is on her way to save you.

Some said it was destiny.
I say I still don't believe
destiny knew anything
about what I thought it would be.

So the story goes.

You would surely leave me
to dwell
remembering innocence of youth.

In my garden always,
you left me
to dwell beneath the silver moon.

So the story goes.

Some people believe
some never see
the dark side of the sun

before the day is done.

I believe you were never happy
with your dreams,
and didn't think you'd find just one.

And so—

Even though I loved you,
there was nothing I could do.
I couldn't change you.

So the story goes.

You would surely leave me
to dwell,
remembering innocence of youth.

In my garden of always.
My garden of always.

Until one day,
I bloomed.

- Age 16

Water Into Wine

Like yesterday's faded sunset
that took away the horizon,
you're a faint memory lost in time.
In the back of my mind, the past rises
to the surface of my soul,
bringing back those
lost words
and empty regrets.
With bittersweet pain
washed by rain,
like tears from my eyes,
I remember yesterday—
when you could turn water into wine.

You used to be my savior,
taking me to new dawns,
like fresh dew on grass where
I stepped with bare feet.
You made the morning dew warm for me.

I was your young and hopeful dreamer,
and you were the brightest star in my sky,
who could always turn
my water into wine.

But pure love can turn bittersweet.
You never were who you
wanted to be,
and my sight was clouded
by your window of lies
that tore us apart

and left me to die.

But all things—
even pain—
must come to an end
and I found
new ways to live.

So now, I remember it
as if it were
yesterday's faded sunset
that took away the horizon,
in the back of my mind,
the past rises—
and rushes through my soul
into the blood in my veins,
leaving
a tingling on my
bare feet
on morning dew.

On my own I'll learn—
to make my own water into wine.

- Age 16

Fear

*Fear is but
a disillusion
an empowerment
that can paralyze
the gift God has given you.*

Life.

*Live it.
Breath it
Be it
Do not be afraid
for the Lord did not intend
living
to be fearful.*

*Embrace trials
embrace pain
and God will bless you —
stronger.*

- Age 16

October Moon

I spent a lifetime knowing you.
Up early in the morning,
talk as your coffee brewed.
I listened to all those things you said,
though I was too young to
understand.
I knew you were my hero.

A man whose hands—
had seen blisters and scars.
They saved the world
and found their way back home.
A man whose feet traveled,
through the muck and mud and tears—
waiting for God to bless you
for your sweat and blood.

I've spent a lifetime missing you.
I look up to the sky,
and wonder if you are there.
All those things you said—
I remember them.
I carry our wisdom in my pocket,
your strength in my hands.

And I sit and wait and remember:
Watching you sleep—
hearing you laugh.
I sit and wait and remember:
the suspender tan lines on your back.

And as a child I would try on your old boots;
they always were too big.
And now as I've grown
I wonder:
would I have had the strength to walk in your
shoes?

You were there a lifetime,
and then you were gone.

But you are in my heart.
Your blood pumps through my veins.
As my soul sets out wandering…
beneath the star-stained sky.

My eyes search for the October moon.

When the air is cold and brisk,
I look to the night sky,
I see the moon ablaze —
and know.

October Moon.

- Age 17

The Poet's Prayer

*Lord it is Your whispered words I hear
as my pen meets my paper,
writing the triumphs and glories of life
as they fall upon my soul.
The simplest things
become the most important virtues.*

*I write to feel it
to see it
to touch it
to smell it
to be it.*

*The miraculous gift you have blessed me with
is great and powerful,
for the words I write
are whispered from the angels,
from You
written so beautiful
to touch the souls of mankind.*

*Thank You Lord for this gift.
Thank You for Your words.*

- Age 17

Time

Time, time—
there is no time.
Too much time
not enough time
too early for time
Whoever said time
meant everything?

I sit
I walk
I run
and still no time.

So stressed.
What's wrong?

I feel as if I am falling into the
black hole under myself,
where eternity stretches to where I can't see.
The world is sucking me into the whirlwind.
The sky is falling on my head.

Where is time when you need it?
Too late—still in bed.

Try, try.
All I do is try.
Try for time.
Try for five things to achieve in this life.
to love
to live

to laugh
to give
to leave my legacy
on this life I live.

But what if I fail?
What if I die?
What if tomorrow is too late?
What happened to all that time?

Will I fly?
Will I crash?
Will I succeed or will I
smash
every bit of hope and dream I hold?
Do you think I can make it on my own?

I want to be brave.
I want to be bold.
I want to
break out of the habit
my everyday holds.

Same thing, same thing
day after day.
I really think it's
time for a change.

So time, time,
I pray to you tonight.

King of hope
King of time

give me strength.
Give me pride.

And I shall not want for time.

- Age 17. I forgot I wrote this poem and found it
years later, after writing my novel, ALL
THESE THREADS OF TIME. It feels like the
beginning of that story swirling in my mind
so long ago . . . always contemplating time!

Gelassenheit
(The Little Things That Save Us)

Tiny little things—
things you never think
always seem to be
the ones that save us from the fink.
Insignificant.
Unknowingly ignored.
Always the ones that save us
from the storm.

Gelassenheit.
Gelassenheit.
Save me now.
Where is what I ignored–
the little thing
that will help me now?

I've cried, I've tried
I've met defeat.
I've met with trial
and deceit.
I've looked and looked
at the familiar,
the obvious
and broad
point of view.

Where is the tiny thing I missed?
Did I miss it in you?

- Age 17

FROM A FRIEND *(JESUS)*

. . .

Dear Friend,

How are you? I just had to send a note to tell you how much I care about you.

I saw you yesterday as you were talking with your friends. I waited all day, hoping you would want to talk with Me, too. I gave you a sunset to close your day and a cool breeze to rest you—and I waited. You never came. It hurt Me, but I still love you, because I am your friend.

I saw you sleeping last night and longed to touch your brow, so I spilled moonlight upon your face. Again, I waited, wanting to rush down so we could talk. I have so many gifts for you! You woke and rushed off to work. My tears were in the rain.

If you would only listen to Me! I love you. I try to tell you in blue skies and in quiet green grass. I whisper it in the leaves on the trees and breathe it in the colors of flowers. I shout it to you in mountain streams, and give the birds love songs to sing. I clothe you with warm sunshine and perfume the air with nature's scents. My love for you is deeper than the ocean and greater than the biggest need in your heart.

Ask Me. Talk with Me. Please don't forget Me. I have so much to share with you.

I won't trouble you any further. It is your decision. I have chosen you, and I will wait—because I love you.

Your Friend,
JESUS

- Age 17 Author's Note: I had forgotten I wrote this. Two decades later, my mother read it at a family funeral. I asked her about it, because I thought it was beautiful. She responded, "You wrote it," and handed me the paper I had written it on decades before. Sometimes, as artists, we may forget the works we've created— and even our own art can touch our hearts again, years later.

Our Lord

*His breath is our heartbeat,
His tears, the morning dew.
His dreams, His creation,
His sky, the canvas
where He paints
The world's dreamscapes.*

*The writer whose words
dance at the reality
Of their truth.*

*The mathematician, the scientist—
He is these too,
As He is the musician
Of the melody of the wind and waves,
birds and gentle human voices.*

*The sculptor who molds us,
the teacher from which we learn,
the key to our hearts
and our souls . . .*

*His breath is our heartbeat,
His will becomes our desire,
because He is Lord.
He is breath.
He is love.*

- Age 18 and published originally by Broken
Streets, *a religious journal in the late 90s.*

Horizon

On the edge of destiny,
I wait.
By my side are my dreams,
packed in an old suitcase.
Pride hides in my pocket.

The world is black here—
silence
that turns me deaf,
exhaustion
leaving my soul drained
when I think about the things
that once tried
to slowly kill me.

But I shall not waste my time
on things that keep one's spirit tame.
Instead, I choose to look into the distance,
beyond the new horizon,
where dreams lie
and hope prevails.

- Age 19

Canary

*The canary is in the cage,
on her perch,
singing.*

*The cage looks
all too familiar.
Through the bars,
beyond her chamber,
she sees a place
exotic,
and she'd like to fly there.*

*She wonders
what it's like
to spread one's wings
and soar.
There is no room
on her perch,
no space in the cage
for flying.
She can only swing
back and forth,
her song her only solace.*

*Oh, to open the door
and be
a canary flying.*

- Age 19

Reach

Reach
Believe
Aspire
Become
All that
lies deep
and true
to your being
your spirit
and your heart.

- Age 19

In Existence

live
breathe
hope
be
become
aspire
rise
steady yourself
find clarity
peace
love
—in existence.

- Age 19

Twenty and Becoming

Space

*There is
a space
that lies
deep
and far
between us
separating
in silence
so sad.*

- Age 20

Mr. Dream Keeper

Mr. Dream Keeper,
what have you done with my dreams?
I held on to them so tightly,
but you've still taken them from me.
Were they not good enough?
Did they not satisfy
the stars I wished on
in the deep black sky?
I need to know, Mr. Dream Keeper—
where have you run to hide?
You see, I had plans and hopes;
I knew exactly, precisely,
how I was to live my life.
Mr. Dream Keeper,
you're really a thief.
You've stolen my hopes,
run away with broken dreams.
What do you want from me?
Is it to be happy? Is it to succeed?
Well, those were my dreams
until you took them from me.
I guess there must be a reason
my aspirations have knocked me off my feet.
I guess I was too busy
dreaming for someone else,
not me.
Now, Mr. Dream Keeper—
now I see.

- Age 20

Belly

*I have been waiting for you
to become
like a fish in my belly
swimming
only to make me nauseous
and spit you out—*

setting us both free.

- Age 20

Poverty

The stink of poverty is suffocating.
It's more than dirty walls and tattered floors
It's tired hands
and tired hearts—
that sink and muddle in despair.

- Age 20

Butterfly

Fly.
Fly.
Freedom calls—
you finally made it
after all.
Beautiful,
spread your wings.
The sky awaits
with wonderful things.

Fly.
Fly.
The sun is smiling.
Despite the rain—
you've come
shining.
Beautiful,
spread your wings.
It's time to soar,
to be.

Butterfly.

- Age 20

Pray

*We should always
pray
the way we do
in a crisis.*

- Age 20

Away

*Down
I dive
(I am not afraid)
I cannot swim
(Tonight I can)
Gracefully,
under water,
I move as if
I am ballet.*

*Time is still
or moving slowly.
Anxieties
do not exist,
and I
find peace in
solitude—
an underwater fantasy
where the sky
is a universe
in space,
away.*

A Lie

*A lie
is something
like
the truth—
backwards.*

- Age 20

He Had a Way About Him

*He had a way about him
that, when you looked in his eyes,
you thought you saw angels flying.*

*He had a way with words,
a way he said things
that made you laugh and think
at once.*

*On solid stones he placed his feet—
a stone statue with
a beating heart,
pumping blood through
his veins.*

*He stood for power and dignity,
intelligence and strength.
He drove
fancy cars
and had expensive gadgets,
the things of the world we crave
and ache for.
He wanted for nothing
but God.*

*Fast he ran, impatiently with darkness,
terrified of trepidation
and anxious in the light,
racing like wind,
exposing the truth
of his sin.*

They opened their eyes with disbelief,
not knowing or understanding
how the man
with dancing angels in his eyes
rode with the devil.

Yet slowly, but surely,
he sank his clay feet
fast and deep
into quicksand,
craving concrete.

And they questioned his reasons,
searching their minds for understanding,
disturbed by their
lack of wisdom,
wondering—
when did they
place their faith
in clay feet
that held up nothing
but a man, humbled and humiliated
by his own humanity?

- Age 20

**You Are a Tulip Tree
(I am an Oak)**

*You are a tulip tree.
You grow straight and tall.
You are rare among trees;
trying to be—
the tallest of all.*

*I am the oak tree,
my roots embedded deep
into the earth.
My branches sway
on strong, windy days—
but what harm is there
in bending with the wind
when the wind is strong?*

*After all, we are both trees;
neither of us is a
birch.
Yet when the cold sets in
and we are naked our leaves,
I wonder—
what is it
you think of me?*

Sad Boy

*Sad boy
with his cigarette,
contemplates life
over a bottle of rum,
some vodka,
accompanied by
an overwhelming feeling
of lost hope.*

- Age 20

Lucy

*She is young
and waiting
for something
anything—
to be
her own.*

- Age 20

Little Girl

Little girl,
your eyes—
big and blue.
The world is bright
and ready for you.
Don't lose your way;
keep your head held high.
You'll always succeed
when you are brave enough
to try.

- Age 21

Quietly

Go away quietly…
Shush.
I can't bear to think of you.
Just leave me alone.
Go away.
Let me be,
to live my life
and remember you like
a movie I once saw,
a dream I once dreamt.
It's better that way—
I can't bear to hear your noise.

- Age 21

Woman in Pink

Drunk on misery,
she sits—
skirt slit high
exposing
new thin legs
naked from the fat
that once clung to them.

Pretty in pink,
Waiting for a man,
as she
smokes her cigarette.

I'm wondering
what gives her the most
satisfaction–
the puffing,
or blowing circles of smoke,
and how long
she will sit
in loneliness
and wonder why.

- Age 21

A Woman's Poem

Are my hips like Barbie?
My breasts—
big and firm,
like Pamela Lee?
Is this all that matters?

Is my hair perfect?
My skin peaches and cream?
Am I a solid 10
on your top-ten rate?
Is this all that matters?

Do I wonder if I'm smart enough?
Do I know if I'm brave?
Can I design a car
or fly into space?
Does this matter to you?

Or would you rather I
Concentrate on my hips
While you gaze at my breasts?

A matter of ignorance
and insecurity.

Dreamer Girl

*There she goes
off to California,
where blonde hair
and Gucci
make dreams come true.*

- Age 21

A Poet's Thoughts

If I see the world
through words and stanzas,
poetry that lives
with its own beating heart,
what do the rest see?
Am I only exposing
the truth of their eyes
and hearts,
the obvious
that lies
before us,
but unspoken
between us?

-Age 21

The Writer

I am—
addicted to my paper,
my pen,
my words,
my thoughts,
my recollections.

Is that what a writer is?

I am not breathing;
I do not exist
without
writing.

Is it a tragedy?
I can express myself
so well with the pen,
yet not so well
in person.

Or is it a blessing
that I can express this
human experience
simply
by playing with words?

- Age 21

Those Certain Girls

I wish I were one
of those certain girls.
The kind with perfect hair,
each cuticle lying flat,
exposing brilliant shine.
The ones with
perfectly painted faces
and manicured nails.
Those certain girls—
you know the ones.
Eyes and lips defined,
breasts perky,
tummies flat.
They are tall and elegant,
tan and toned,
every piece of clothing
perfectly tailored—
stylish,
trendy.
Men gasp when they walk by.
She becomes
the topic of conversation.
Those girls.
Those certain girls.

- Age 21

On Growing Up

*We have found ourselves
wandering under a selfless sky,
stretching far and wide
for our view.
We walk miles together
and apart,
and push ahead.
We call ourselves grownups
because we've gone to college,
paid the rent,
maybe we've even
gotten married
or had babies.
But it wasn't long ago
that we screamed at pep rallies
and fought over beer and boys—
and rumors.
How quickly we change
when life goes on,
and we find ourselves
standing silent,
wondering—
where did the time go?*

- Age 21

Silence

Silence can say nothing
and everything at once.
You need to be willing
to listen.
Then you will understand:
Sometimes there is nothing to say,
and only silence
can say what you mean
to tell.
Only silence
finds the words.

Hot Shot

Three dollars in my pocket,
the heat is hot today—
one hundred degrees and rising.
But the wind is cold
where you stand
on your mountain.
I will only look up to see you;
you ignore my call.
Maybe you are just
too high
to hear.

- Age 22

A Child

A child can dream of becoming a hero
and grow up to be a Nazi.
He can be smart, gifted with intelligence,
and become
the Unabomber.
He can strive to be perfect
and impressive,
and become an ignorant fool.
Be aware
of what you teach your children:
their dreams are fragile,
vulnerable
to the world they live in.

- Age 22

History

Some of us
change the times.
Others
ride the wings,
follow along
to the next beat,
the next step—
into what will someday
be seen
as
revolutionary.

- Age 23

Will

They said,
"You can't."

I said,
"I will."

And then—
I did.

- Age 23

Her Light

*The light is still on
in her room.
It flickers
over scattered CDs,
pretending to be
busy and used.
She left the light on
as a reminder
of her life,
her love,
her journey—
before she moved on.*

- Age 23

**Just How Much
(Jesus Loves Me)**

*Jesus and I
stroll through the garden
of splendor and delight,
past the daisies and the roses,
past cherubim by the gate.
His hand in mine,
His eyes a gentle gaze,
His voice soft and sweet
as I hear Him say,
"Child, do you know how I have loved you?"*

*I have no answer,
only sorrowful tears in my eyes.
Then, as I find my voice,
I quietly reply,
"You saved me, Lord, and made me new.
Though my selfish heart has been deceived,
the world has tried to empty it
and take my soul away from You.
Sometimes I find myself falling,
feeling empty,
though in my heart
I have always known Your love
and have kept my faith.
If You can, forgive me
for all I have failed."*

*I look away after speaking these words,
feeling like a disgrace.
But then, in that moment,*

my Savior's gaze
turns my eyes to His.
He holds my hand more tightly,
His eyes brighter than the stars,
His voice more beautiful
than the song of dawn.
He looks at me and says,
"My precious dear, I have always loved you.
When you cry, I cry too.
When you face temptation, I understand.
I have never left your side.
Though the world has tried, it has failed.
It cannot steal me from your heart.
My child,
you are imperfect and human,
but your faith in Me
is what has saved you.
Because of your faith,
you have been forgiven."

It is then
that I fall into my Savior's embrace
and rest in His arms.
I understand the meaning of grace,
and know
just how much
Jesus loves me.

Henry Sunshine

There once was a man
named Henry.
Henry Sunshine,
that's what they called him.
He wore old blue Dickies
and a buttoned shirt,
half-tucked in,
black New Balance shoes, size 9E—
always slightly crooked,
because he walked on the inside of each foot.

Every day,
he walked up and down Main Street
with his cane.
Along his journey,
he'd stop in every shop
to say, "Hello!"
Sometimes it was hard to understand him,
his words slurring a bit.

He was simple
and beautiful,
and I looked forward to seeing him
each day at 3:00,
in the shoe department where I worked.

He'd come in and say,
"You're a real humdinger, woman!"
(He called all the girls humdingers.)
Henry always claimed
all the women were after him.

Once, on a cloudy day,
we asked Henry where the sunshine was.
He pointed to his baseball cap,
which he wore every day.
It said, Henry Sunshine,
in big red letters across the front.
He then replied,
"The sunshine is on my hat!"

Good old Henry Sunshine—
that humdinger.
He's the finest man in town.

The Light

A flame burns inside you—
don't let it go.

Know how it moves and flickers,
naked of the world,
bare in God's skin.

Let it dance,
for without it,
your light is dim.

Shadow

Sleep shadow
Rest and wait
Until you are
Brave enough
To go
Your own way.

Searching for Truth

There's a truth
that lies
within the web of deceit.
Untangle the web,
and you will find yourself—
a genius of the obvious,
and simple.
You will know
that true understanding
is not a virtue
of the ignorant
but a realization
of an open mind.

Out of the Box

Dare to dream.
Strive to live.
Color outside the lines.
All that you are
is you.
All that you answer to
is yourself and God.
Being all you can be
is not being all they expect.
To know your true self
is to step outside the box,
leaping with faith.

Brighter

Be joyful in every day.
Look to the sky and cry,
"Thank you!"
The life you live
Is that of which you make it.
The love that extends from your hands,
Your heart,
Your smile,
Is the love that comes back to you
Stronger and dignified.
Waste no time on nonsense—
Worrying about nonsense only brings
Nonsense.
Reap faith,
And goodness will come.
Expect it.
Be ready for it.
Embrace it,
And the light inside you
Will shine
Brighter.

Stranger

There you go, stranger,
someone I once knew.
The stones in your eyes
burn cold,
waiting to set sail
on the moon.

And you talk—
your eyes wander
(never looking me in the eye).
Is that
the pain you feel,
the suffering?
Does speaking to me
hurt your pride?

Well, I've lain awake
a thousand and one nights,
wondering
what has filled your heart
so empty inside.

Nothing comes to mind.

So walk away, stranger.
I will bite my tongue
and know that you
understand
(even if you do not admit)
the cost your pride
has done.

Lay Still

*Lay still this night
and know,
I love you.*

Dance Me to the Moon

Dance me to the moon,
Sway me to the beat of you.
Let all be forgotten
And all forgiven,
For it is only you I seek,
And only you I breathe.

Dance me to the moon,
Spin me to the stars,
Where weightless we leap
And endless we gaze
Upon the eyes
Of a burning love
That is profound and brave.

For I need a love
That is tender and bright,
A rock on which to stand.
It is you I seek in the depths of night
When all is dark and gray.

And in this place,
Where hunger tests and turns
In the seat of my starving soul,
I thirst for your embrace,
Your thoughts,
For your words are my wine.

So dance me to the moon, my darling,
Sway me to the beat of you,

For I have been told
There are stars
That never lose their shine.

- Age 23

Let's Just Get Married

Let's just get married.
Let's get married tonight.
Should we call the
justice of the peace
or fly to Vegas?
I don't care.

Let's just get married.
I don't need a wedding.
I don't care about
the fancy dress,
the reception buffet,
or even the fancy gifts
and cards.

I just want to be your wife,
want to call you my husband,
rub your sore back
with cold clay
that tingles your veins,
cut your hangnails,
and kiss you
with soft, tender lips.

I want to press my hand in yours
and learn the quiet ways
you carry the world—
to journey through life with you
like the carnival ride
I was too afraid to try,
but never once regretted.

Let's just get married.
Let's vow to take care
of one another
here and now.

I will love you always.
Why should we wait?

Let's just get married.
Let's get married tonight.

The Fruit

Look to love,
look to God, not hate.
The hand that feeds you
can also poison you.
Remember: lips that speak
only cover teeth that bite.
The fruit you eat
runs through your body,
spreading nutrients and vitamins,
giving health and growth.
Eat the temptations,
and you'll find yourself
greedy and fat.
Indulgence leaves you empty,
and you never know
why you are so unhappy.
Step back, look on.
Dreams can be sweet
when you know
which fruit to taste.

The Mountain Climb

*A man once said: "It's not the view from the top;
    it's the climb that brings the most satis-
    faction."*

*He told a story of a man who climbed to the
    highest peak. Each step was accomplish-
    ment, like a badge on his coat, a trophy on
    the shelf, waiting for oohs and ahs. Yet,
    when he stood at the top of the mountain,
    he couldn't remember how he got there.*

*I think of this as I sit at the bottom, gazing at the
    peak. I decide to spend more time noticing
    the scenery, letting my arms and legs get
    muddy. With each climb, look within myself;
    I look out to God. When I reach the top, I
    look down—not remembering the "oohs and
    ahs," but the dirt, grime, and sweat that
    brought me to this place.*

*Where the view is my freedom, and the climbing
    —a part of my character.*

Thirty Something

Woman

I am a woman.
I was born a girl.
I wore pigtails
and clothes too big for dress-up.
Then I grew up.

I am a woman.
I am the housekeeper,
the chef,
the baker,
sometimes the doctor,
the accountant.
I tend the tending.

I am a woman.
I am expected to be
everything.
I have my career—
I take care of that.
I come home.
I don't stop.
I cook.
I clean.
I kiss boo-boos.
I get lunches made,
clothes laid out,
baths done.

The telephone's ringing.
The cat is hissing.
The children are crying.

The dinner is burning…

I am not God,
But apparently, I'm to be everything—
to everyone
all at once.

I am a woman.
I was born a girl,
and I'm wondering—
where is me?

Spinning in Space

Aren't we all just spinning in space,
floating—
searching,
trying to find our place?

Waiting for the world to begin,
waiting for the world to end.

Waiting in line
to pass the time,
wearing a mask like a Stepford wife,
our skin hiding the same bones inside,
our hearts on the shelf
to spite our pride.

Isn't it all just a game—
words that hurt,
words that taunt,
words that blame,
spinning around,
pointing fingers of shame?

I've been waiting
for something beautiful.

Guess I was a fool,
waiting on the world.

I've been looking
for something beautiful.

Who knew
all along
I already had it in you?

I've stood at the bottom,
gazed at the top.
I've climbed.
I've bled.
I've fallen.
Oh, the tears I've shed.

I've fallen down—
broken.

I never waited for Superman,
but oh, how I hoped.

You

You,
You with those judgmental eyes
staring down at me.
You and my hands scorned as I scrubbed the
frying pan too hard and too long.

You with the smell of Chantilly
that made my nose sting.
You who are every part of so many things
I say and do.

You.

You with those words of advice as you
sipped your tea
While I drummed my fingers on the table
wishing you'd stop.
You with your crying and your yelling and your
dark rooms
And your quiet anger simmering under the door.
Your laughter.
Your long silences pulling at puppet strings.

You.

You and all those things that made you
the you I knew.
You and all those things they say you
were before I knew you.
You and all the fears you instilled in me.
And the courage you taught me.

Yes, you.

We're still blaming you.

Who do you blame?
What do you shame?
Who said you had to be perfect?
Who said I did?
Who says any of us are?

You. Yes, you.

But the one staring down in judgment—
Is me.

Maybe
I should let you go.

Glow

Light of blue glows
in the dark room

She's gone.
And on TV, people are living life
like life goes on.

And I remember.

I peek at her through the door crack
I want to scream and shout
but I can't say a word

The silence between us
is too loud

Love's Light

The light of love
Cannot be seen or touched
Only felt
And given.

The Writer's Poem

I am a writer.
I write.

I pound away at keys
on my MacBook Pro.
I write in journals
and on napkins.

I write with coffee and tea
and chocolate cake
and popcorn.

Sometimes I fall asleep writing.

Sometimes I stare at the blank screen
and feel sick.

The blinking cursor
taunts me.

I am a writer.

What do I write?

Everything.

But mostly I agonize over characters
that squirm around in my head, teasing me,
demanding to control the page—
unwilling and never quiet,
like spoiled children.

Stories whirl and twirl,
turning me upside down
and inside out.

Yes, I'm a writer.

I'm the quiet one
watching and listening,
not really present in this conversation
because I'm too busy noticing
the way the sun casts a glow on your face,
the way your voice cracks when you talk,
the funny way you bite your lip.

No job is really suited for me.
I'm always just a little too far away—
much happier lost in the page
than by the chatter
at the water cooler.

Even if that conversation
might inspire a story.

You won't understand me.

Unless you write.

Especially if I can't hand you
a magazine or journal you've heard of
with my name inside.
You won't understand
why I'm pounding away at the keyboard
late at night
or lost in the blue glow

of a screen.

Words have danced wildly in my head
since I was old enough
to run my fingers across the pages
of Mother Goose
and Little Golden Books.

Twisting.
Molding.
Scraping each page,
each line,
word by word—
building, painting, shouting out
all that is deep and buried
and waiting
to be heard.

I am a writer.

I write
with perfect insanity—
and never-ending grace.

Winter

Bitter cold
Pierces and numbs the skin
Stabbing sharp
Like knives
Through every cell of my flesh.

The light of day
Can be seen
But I
Feel no warmth
From the sun

Only bitter cold
Until Spring comes.

Witness (The Death of a Boy, 1986)

I think of him sometimes—
The ten-year-old boy swinging his arms,
stretching his long, lanky legs,
his socks pulled up to his knees.

He drags the shovel across the railroad tracks
and picks up a spike.
The sun casts a shadow on his face.

I look behind him
at the canopy of oaks and pines.
Our dog is buried there.

I remember him, sometimes.
Thirteen, crying in the kitchen doorway—
grass-stained knees, baseball jersey torn.

He yells louder than Dad.
Their voices tremble in my gut.
The yelling is too much.

I cover my eyes. I peek.
Through the cracks of my fingers, I see—

he dodges Dad's clenched fist.
Stunned, Dad leaves.

Baseball is gone forever.

I know him, this boy.
He sat next to me at the kitchen table,

passing salt and pepper,
sipping Mountain Dew,
pretending everything was okay.

He thought his pain went unnoticed.

But I noticed.

I witnessed
the death of that boy
In 1986.

Take Me to the River

Take me to the river
Take me to the stream
Take me to the water
And let it wash over me.

Stop the ground from shaking
From swallowing me
I'm reaching for Your hand, Lord
Set me free.

Take me to the water,
Because now I see
Sometimes, that's just the way it be.

So come on and rescue me.

Jesus, Lift Me

Jesus, lift me
Jesus, heal me
Jesus, be with me
Under the tree
We have so much to talk about.

Jesus, help me
Jesus, show me
I've counted the cost
Of the cross.

Forgive them for what they do not see—
I have not always seen.

Jesus, see me
Carry me.

Every cell in my body glorifies You.

I Am Coming

Be still.
I am coming—
like a freight train,
thunder rolling.

I hear it inside.
Wait for it.
I have not gone away.

I have been wrapped up,
swaddled like a newborn,
hunched in my cocoon,
growing,
pushing,
bending,
shedding my skin,
becoming new.

I am coming,
because I have finally become.

The Law Graduate

I stood long by the window
of the seventh floor,
looking out at the patriot city—
revolutionary,
cobblestone and history—
past the old stone church
and the glass skyscraper windows.
Sun peeked in, casting glare
on the mahogany desk.
I did not feel a chill.
I did not think,
Wow, look at me here.
Nor did I step outside myself
and wonder,
Who the hell am I?
No—
I was comfortable in my skin.
I had earned it.
The becoming had occurred.
I had embarked on the final stretch,
the steps behind me
suddenly making sense—
nothing insignificant.
I realized then
when something is meant to be
you know it.
It falls into place,
because God's plan
is perfect like that.

So I Could Fly

It feels like a death.
I stand on the edge of the mountain,
The one I spent forever climbing—
day by day,
year by year,
one stump at a time.

I stare down at the world beneath me:
tiny
unrecognizable.
distant.

I shut my eyes—
steady on one foot.
hold my breath.
It's a long way down.
I wait for the fall.

But wait!
Something stops me.
What? I don't know.

I open my eyes.
I see it:
A wider view,
bigger than the mountain.
The sky.

It's all so clear!
All the trudging,
Dragging one foot in front of the other,

tripping on rocks,
stomach cramped, out of breath—

It was not so I could stand at the top,
rested,
admiring the view.

No.

I climbed so I could jump,
find wings where I had none.

So I could fly.

Forty and Forward

Remember!

Remember!
To be alive!
The sun hot,
The birds bold,
The moment NOW.

The sky stretched wide and blue,
Whispering of something true.
While hose sprayed rainbows,
Leave drops of glass on grass
Like morning dew.

Oh, to remember
To be alive,
Living loud.

For the world may quarrel,
But let no such quarrel reach your heart.

Sub Zero

Cold.
Still.
Night.
The world—
paused.
In frozen tundra,
waiting—
to be warmed.

Even Raindrops

Even raindrops
On trees
Have their own
Song:
A tap-tap on the leaves,
Leftover morning dew,
Rhythmic like
The tip-pity tap
Of a high school boy's pencil on his desk.
He's going to be a rockstar—
If only for today.

The Ocean

Pushing and pulling,
keeper of unforgiving secrets—
where lives have been lost
along sandy beaches
as children play.

Starfish wash ashore,
stranded
then taken back
as waves collapse to sand,
the tide orchestrating—

wiping clean
all that was yesterday,
ready
to start again.

Lovecraft's Providence

In distant spaces,
time lapsed.
Iron gates and street lanterns,
now gone dark—
in vacant lands
of earth,
where landscapes shift,
but skylines, sometimes,
remain the same.

Here, on these steps of the observatory—
a young boy dreamed stories far and wide,
fantastical inklings of his heart,
yet to be told to the world.

Now, standing on these steps,
separated only by time and space—
I stare at the door,
understanding, for the first time,
how the curiosities of life
entangle us—
and also set us free.

Manifest

Remember:
candlelight dreams
summoning the universe
in dark corners
where hope crept in.

Word by word,
line by line,
a life unfolding—
kept in moments,
fevered by vision—
of things not lived
yet breathing
now, all at once.

Someday, yesterday—
an eternal, widening space
that stretches thin
then gathers itself
into view.

Being all it is,
all you are,
dancing in corners,
waiting to sing—

into light.

So sing.
Manifest.
The world waits to hear.

Oblivious

People move
oblivious to being watched.
Now—we have cameras in traffic lights.

I go to Walmart
The greeter at the door never smiles,
while the symphony of register beats
keeps time
with the rolling of my cart.

In Silence

In all that you do,
find silence.
Breathe.

Let your mind wander
Step off the race.

God lives in the silence.

Box

I do not fit in a box.

Not my words, my ideas, my aspirations.
Not my musings or imagination.
Nor my dreams, desires or memories.
Not my fears, talents, or hopes—
Or any other snapshot of me.

I am full.
I am wide.
I am vast.
I am strong.

I am everything my Creator made me—
And still becoming more.

I am wanting.
I am seeking.
I am learning.
I am changing.

Each day.
Each moment.
Every second.

I do not fit in a box.

Stop trying
to push me in.

Done and Said

It's all been said before.

Words of heartbreak.
Pain.
Loss.

You hurt me.
How dare you
I hate you
Am I not good enough?

You judge me.
You weren't there.
Do you love me?

So many faces, places and moments—
escaped from lips
bled from hearts
again
and again.

Pain that bleeds,
smolders,
begging for answers.

It's all be done before.

Leaving.
Going away.
Dying.
Sick.

Saying goodbye—
Not enough time.

Boasting,
selfish.

Somewhere a selfless heart,
Seeks something good,
searches for the why.

What is wrong with me?

It's all been said.
It's all been done,

But I won't be prisoner to it.

Not anymore.

Dandelion

Everybody wants to be somebody.
They don't know
They already are.

Because somebody can be anybody,
And that someone
Is exactly who you are.

Everybody wants to be some place
Other than right here, right now.
But some place can be this place,
Not just dreams on faraway stars.

Maybe who you are, and where you are,
Is exactly where you need to be
To learn and grow and discover
So the you of tomorrow
Will be ready to meet "me."

Because who you are is changing,
Even if you don't see it yet.
Like wishes wished on dandelions,
The seed has blown—
It's already been set.

Tune In

Tune in,
Or tune out.
But either way—
Tune up your heart.

Soundtrack

The stirring whir of my mother's womb,
the rushing brook,
keeping rhythm to my father's breath
as we walk.

The stillness of night
as I gazed upon your face,
the sound of my fingers digging into the earth
as I planted.

And she sings.

Clouds move—I watch, but do not hear.
I feel my child's tiny hands,
And hear the trickle of water
As it starts to boil,
the teapot whistle, a warning.

The sound of my pen on the paper—
A reminder: I am alive.

Close your eyes and remember:
the rustle of leaves,
the ocean swept to the sand,
A cricket's song in June.

A soundtrack to a life lived—
out loud,
in silence.

Still listening.

Hair

*Tiny strands
down the drain,
swept up
by a hairdresser's broom.*

*Clinging to my brush,
my shirt,
my car—
scattered to the wind,
remade
in a bird's nest,
a squirrel's bed.*

*Caught in a comb,
kept—
tied with a bow:
the ponytail
I cut at ten.*

*Hair that holds
the secrets of my DNA,
and traces
of every color,
every perm—*

every past self.

Ode to My Belly

Ode to my belly—
Once flat,
never a six-pack,
but
two babies instead.

Stretched like Gumby,
a superpower—
making room
for life.

Then shrinking back,
though marked
with wrinkled,
leftover skin
and the fading days
of belly chains,
once worn proud.

But still—
the belly button
that tied life in.

Family Face

They are —
faces seen,
faces remembered.

I see
my eyes in theirs
and carry —

my mother's nose,
my grandmother's cheeks,
my father's thick hair.

We are moving DNA,
lit by a spark —
a new story,
with the same heart.

The Best is Yet to Come

I am still in the basement,
sometimes.

I hear stomping feet above me.
I need to pee, but I, hold it in,
too afraid to go up.

I am still staring at the hole
in the bathroom floor,
sometimes.

I measure my value there.
Will I ever make it?
Does it mark my worth—
my destiny?

I am still in the hospital bed,
sometimes.

The IV is dry.
My veins burn.
Can the doctors fix me?
I am too young to die.

I am still in the corner,
sometimes.

Heart thumping,
Mind racing.
Will this anxiety end?
Will the walls stop closing in?

And then, one day,
I am no longer there.

I sit across the table.
"We no longer need you," she says.

But what I hear is:
You are not enough.

So I drive.

And somewhere between
where I was
And where I am going,
I decide—

This is not the end of my story.

I'm not there anymore.

I am here.

On my knees.
Grateful for the past.

You can't pray for a better one.

The best is yet to come.

Oh, To Save You

Oh, to save you.
Wouldn't that be something grand?

Show you the patterns, so easy,
so you could see.
Stop repeating them.
Stop being them.
Beat them.

Oh, to save you.
What I would give.

Write you a story, a song, a poem.
A speech about how to
let it all go.

Put it up in bright lights.
Show you on the screen.
Sit and pray and hope
you see the things I see.

But instead, we'll go round about it
another time again.

And I'll get choked up
every time the phone rings,
worried it's about you.
Worried I might not see you
again.

Oh, to save you.

What I'd give.

*But I guess
all I can do is
save myself.*

*Can barely
save myself.*

Sandy

She's got paper and pencil,
a vision etched in graphite.
I watch it come to life
at four, maybe five.

She's got soil and shovels,
her violets bloom—
in sunshine and rainbows
sometime in June.

She's chaotic,
she's crying
her hair in a ball—
I'm afraid she's dying.
I hear her cry through the wall.

She's one drink of vodka
and two hiding under the sink.
I'd tell on her, but
what will everyone think?

She's a smile, she's laughter.
We stay up all night.
She makes me believe in
all the magic
hidden out of sight.

I love her, I miss her.
Hated to see her drift away.
Gone before I got the chance
to say thank you,

and sorry for all we missed,
for all the times I wished I could've stayed.

So instead, I'll remember:
etching our initials in concrete.
We thought the house was haunted—
But turns out—
it was just our family.

A sister, a mother, a friend,
a blood line in cursive and ink.
On adoption papers
we didn't need—

she always belonged.

New England

*New England blood runs through our veins
All the way back to beginning days
When our ancestors steered course to
anchor the ship.*

*And since then, it's been some time
Sitting here, watching leaves die
Remembering when we
Stamped our names in concrete.*

*I'm just one truth away
From a trauma spiral taking over me.*

*And I'm glad you got your therapy
The waiting room white noise
Always got to me
Made me worry it was me
That made you sick.*

*A broken brain can't tell the time
Just stuck in moments passed
And circumstances we didn't pick.*

*The way Dad dreamt of hitting a ball,
but all he got was 'Nam
And now like COVID,
we've been masked far too long.*

What does it all mean?

I try not to contemplate

Instead, I sit with my dog and stare at the sun
He agrees we've been tied up far too long
Waiting for permission to be free—
Oh, to be free.

Till then, I'll walk
in the faded footsteps on this path—
These trees remember more
than we see.

And I finally understand:
You can take me out of New England
But you can't take New England out of me.

In This Life

Fleeting.
Moving.
Passing
through
these moments of time.

Breaking.
Loving.
Feeling.
Waiting.
Drowning
in the tide that pulls us.

Missing.
Hoping.
Longing
for light to find us.

Erasing
all the darkness.

as we reach
for peace.

The Smallest Knight

Once, the smallest knight
set out to save the world
from a fiery monster—
after the girl.

He waited and wished
for the moment to come
when he could find his bravery
in front of everyone.

And when it came,
alas he met
all he'd hoped for,
but hadn't become yet.

Love Letters

*I'm sorry I don't write you love letters
anymore—*

*fleeting words on paper,
bled from the heart,
stamped by the soul,
proclaiming all I feel.*

*But it's all here,
in this heart of mine.*

*In the mornings,
when I look at your face
and kiss your cheeks
and say,
Good Morning!*

*It's when I reach for your hand.
When I talk and sing
nonsense songs
just to make you laugh.*

*It's when I make your tea,
and we talk in the car,
driving somewhere—
Or nowhere—
together.*

*Always on an adventure.
Since day one.*

*I'm sorry I don't write you love letters
on paper.*

*But I write them everyday
in the air—
in the quiet moments,
etched forever
on my heart.*

The Poem

I caught it—
fast
and steady—

As it drifted past
like a silk scarf,
blazing in the wind,
dancing,
taunting,
beautiful.

I didn't want to catch it.
I wanted to let it fly free.
It was too beautiful to take.

But as I watched it disappear,
I realized—

if I didn't grab hold,
grasp it, quick,
clenched between my fingers,

no one could wear it.
No one would feel it
smooth against their skin,
inhale its sweet perfume,
admire how its
warm colors
brighten their cheeks,
their souls.

So, I caught it.

I held it.
I felt it.

I closed my eyes,
I recited it.
I remembered it.

I wrote it down.

Then I let it go,

so someone else
could grab hold too.

Gold-Spun Fingers

Gold-spun fingers
work like sunbeams,
casting light
to the page—

finding their way,
etched in ink,
then slipping loose
into birdsong,
lost to ether.

Lingering,
gone—
but always there.

Generation X Rant

No, I don't want Copilot to write for me.
And I'll keep my em dashes—thank you.

Algorithms know more about me these days,
Then I know about myself.

Remember when the idea of a video call
was The Jetsons
or Back to the Future, Part II*—*
So futuristic.

Now I keep my camera off
And text instead.

Outside—the air makes me feel alive.
Cold in my lungs beneath a blue sky,
sharp like the corners of a crisp white envelope
that make you bleed from paper cuts,
holding important messages,
sealed with saliva on glue,
but never containing the words
in your diary—if you kept one.

Useless, pointless,
and so, so real
until it's not—
just working through
the stuff that keeps us up at night.

The world is moving fast
and I only want to stand still

and watch the way the trees blow in the wind.
Like dancing.
Blowing today like yesterday
and tomorrow.

And my mind settles.

I think about MTV—
even it unplugged.
Isn't it ironic?
The '80s are nostalgic.
And I'm still growing in my eyebrows
from all that over-plucking in '95.

Doesn't it feel like
all that commotion—
Axl Rose vs Vince Neil,
And Debbie Gibson vs Tiffany—
set us up for today's politics
And social media memes?

The ones where we pretend to
stand for only one thing.
No room for grey.

But life is nothing but.

So, no—I don't want Copilot to write for me
And I'll keep my em dashes, thank you.
Because it's the dash between the years
that make a life—
don't you think?

Rebel, Rebel

Hey Rebel, put your jacket on—
the day is short,
the night is long.

Hey Rebel, stop hiding your face—
not everything has to
be put in its place.

Accept what's inside you,
stop hiding behind the wall.
You'll never fly
if you're afraid to fall.

In spaces between,
you can find the hope you lost—
reclaim it again.

Hope to see you, friend.

Rebel, Rebel—
just begin.

Acknowledgments

Thank you to every person who ever encouraged me to write —especially my mother, who made sure I had piles of journals and somehow got me my first computer when we didn't have the money. To every experience that shaped me, and to every writer, artist, musician, or creative soul who ever inspired me: without you, what a lonely world it would be.

A special thank you to Kelsey Gietl for designing the cover. As always, it took my breath away!

A special thank you to all the readers, booksellers, librarians, fellow writers, and others who have been a part of this journey. Your support is awe-inspiring. In stories, a hero must always gather her allies. You are all some of mine.

The rest of my allies? My husband and children—my number ones. They are my biggest cheerleaders. Being a writer is often lonely, filled with doubt, struggle, and mountains to climb to bring work into the world. Their support and sacrifice has brought me here. Brave and ready to be who I always was from the start: a rebel poet. A rebel writer. Always bleeding on the page. Finally, the courage to share it.

Thank you also to the younger me who kept going, kept writing, and never stopped. Her bravery made this book.

Most of all, thank you, God, for the gift of words and the ability to tune into the stories, the wisdom, and the heart that live between the heartbeat of each word.

I truly believe art can change the world. Whether it's poetry, stories, music, or any expression of the human soul, art can save us. It reminds us who we are.

So keep creating. Keep daring. The world needs you. It needs your encouraging words.

Sarah Crowne

About Sarah Crowne

Sarah Crowne writes cinematic speculative thrillers that explore the moments that change everything. Known for stories that grip both the heart and the mind, her books blend suspense, mystery, and emotional depth. She also writes creative nonfiction, poetry, and anything that inspires.

A mentee of John Truby and a Pushcart Prize and Best of the Net nominee, Sarah balances her legal career with a life-long love of storytelling. Known to readers as "A Busy Lady," she believes stories help us ask brave questions—and find strength within ourselves when it matters most.

More From Sarah Crowne

If you enjoyed this book, please consider leaving a review online. To receive updates on new releases and events, sign up for her newsletter at **sarahcrownebooks.com** and check out her other books!

Sylvie Mitchell's world falls apart when her sister is murdered the same night her father vanishes without a trace. Crushed with grief, Sylvie consoles her mother and younger brother alone. But then Sylvie discovers an incredible gift: the ability to time travel. Determined to rewrite the past, she embarks on a desperate quest to save her sister, find her father, and stop the killer terrorizing her once peaceful New England town. Can Sylvie stop the killer before she becomes his next target, or will she alter the fabric of reality trying to put an end to his rage? Set in the late 80s, ALL THESE THREADS OF TIME is a cutting-edge time travel murder mystery that asks, how far would you go to save the ones you love?

Pop sensation Nikki Scott has it all-fame, fans, and a voice that sells out arenas. But when her mother mysteriously dies mid-concert, everything collapses. Left only with her mother's cryptic final words-"Cancel the show"-Nikki sets out for answers. Teaming up with the estranged brother she barely remembers, Nikki uncovers dark family secrets-and a dangerous power stirring within her. As a shadowy organization closes in, intent on weaponizing her voice, Nikki must unravel the truth before she becomes the ultimate instrument of control. The show must go on... but will it end in blood?

Your creative revolution starts now. *After igniting inspiration in Volume I,* Rebel Writers Volume II *takes you deeper—into the lives and minds of America's literary rebels who defied convention and shaped the nation's stories. From the dark corners of Poe's imagination to Thoreau's transcendent woods and Flannery O'Connor's piercing truths, Sarah Crowne uncovers the power behind fearless writing. Are you ready to ignite your own creative fire and write boldly? The pen is in your hand. The rebel legacy awaits.*

For more books and upcoming projects visit
http://sarahcrownebooks.com